Best Bible Stories

The story of Joseph is found
in the Old Testament of the Bible,
in chapters XXXVII to L of Genesis.

The text of this book
has been prepared with reference to:
The Good News Bible (1994),
The New English Bible (1970),
The New Jerusalem Bible (1990),
The Revised Standard Version (1973).

Series editor: Jacqueline Vallon

*The publishers wish to thank
Geoffrey Marshall-Taylor, Educational Consultant,
for his kind help.*

ISBN 1 85103 268 1
© 1997, Gallimard Jeunesse
Illustrations coloured by Anne Gutman
English text © 1998, Moonlight Publishing Ltd
First published in the United Kingdom 1998
by Moonlight Publishing Ltd, 36 Stratford Road, London W8
Printed in Italy by Editoriale Libraria

Best Bible Stories

THE STORY OF JOSEPH

Retold by Clare Best
Illustrated by Maurice Pommier

Moonlight Publishing

In the hills of Canaan, near the town of Hebron, Joseph and his brothers looked after the sheep and goats that belonged to their father, Jacob.
Joseph was a young man of seventeen. He was charming, good-looking and popular. Everyone liked him, everyone except his brothers. They hated Joseph for being their father's favourite.

Jacob made no secret of the fact that he preferred his two youngest sons, Joseph and Benjamin. They reminded him of their mother, Rachel, a wife he had loved dearly. She had died giving birth to their youngest son, Benjamin.

In fact, Jacob loved Joseph more
than any of his other sons. He even
made a long, decorated robe especially
for him. It was a robe fit for a prince.

Joseph's brothers were jealous of him. And Joseph annoyed them when he told their father all that happened each day. He sometimes gave his father bad reports of his brothers...

One morning Joseph told his brothers about a dream he had, and they hated him even more:

"I dreamt we were all in the field tying up sheaves of wheat. My sheaf stood up and all yours bowed down to mine."

In those days dreams were taken very seriously. People believed their dreams carried messages from God, or could foretell the future.

Joseph told his brothers about another of his dreams:

"The sun, the moon and eleven stars bowed down to me."

Even Jacob thought this was going a bit far, and scolded Joseph,

"What kind of a dream is that? Must we all, your mother, your brothers and I, all bow down to you?"

Joseph's brothers grew more and more envious of him and wondered what the future would hold. Would Joseph take what they owned and rule over them? Jacob thought hard about it all.

One day, when Joseph's brothers had
taken their father's flock of sheep to
graze at Shechem, Jacob said to Joseph,
"Go and find out how your brothers
are doing and bring me word."

Joseph set off straightaway. Near Shechem, he met a man who told him that his brothers had moved on to Dothan, so Joseph followed.

Joseph's brothers saw him coming
in the distance. This was the perfect
chance to get rid of their brother.
"Here comes the dreamer. Let's kill
him and throw his body into a dry well.
We'll say a wild beast has eaten him."
But the oldest brother, Reuben, wanted
to save Joseph, and told his brothers,

"Put him in a well, but don't kill him!"
When Joseph reached them, his
brothers pulled his decorated robe off
him and flung him into a dry well.

Then they sat down to eat. Just then,
they saw some merchants on their way
from Gilead into Egypt. Their camels
were loaded with spices, balm and
myrrh. Judah, one of the brothers, said
to the others,
"Our laws forbid us to kill our brother,
and anyway what would we gain? Let's
sell Joseph to these merchants."
The eleven brothers all agreed.

They pulled Joseph out of the well and sold him to the merchants for twenty pieces of silver.
To make it look as though Joseph had been eaten by a wild beast, they killed a goat and smeared its blood on his robe. Then they sent the robe to Jacob with a message, "We found this. Does it belong to your son?" Jacob knew it was Joseph's robe. He fell into a terrible grief for his lost son, blaming himself for letting Joseph travel alone. He tore his clothing, wept for days, and wore sackcloth. No-one could comfort him.

15

Meanwhile, Joseph had been taken to
Egypt and sold as a slave to Potiphar,
who was one of the Pharaoh's officials
and the captain of the palace guard.

But God had not forgotten him. He made
sure Joseph did everything very well.
Potiphar, his master, was really pleased
with Joseph, and put him in charge of his
whole household.

Potiphar's wife had noticed Joseph too.
She thought he was very handsome
and she asked him to make love to her.
But Joseph refused. He would not
betray his master's trust in him. Besides,
he was a Hebrew and he respected
God's law, which forbids love with
another man's wife.
One day when Joseph went into the
house and Potiphar's wife was on her
own, she caught hold of his robe.

"Come to bed with me", she said.
But Joseph ran away from her, leaving
her holding his robe. She called the
servants and showed them Joseph's robe.
"Look at this!" she said, "Joseph came
into my room and tried to attack me,
but when I screamed he ran away."
She told Potiphar the same lies, and he
was so angry that he had Joseph locked
up in prison.

Once again God helped Joseph to do all his work well, so that the jailer was pleased with him. He put Joseph in charge of all the prisoners. Among them were the chief baker, who made bread for the Pharaoh's table, and the chief cupbearer, who tasted the Pharaoh's food and wine. One night, each of them had a dream.

In the morning, Joseph saw that the two
men were upset, and asked them why.
The cupbearer told him,
"I dreamt of a vine with three branches.
The leaves came out, the blossoms
opened and the grapes ripened. I held the
Pharaoh's cup, squeezed the grapes into
it and and put the cup into his hand."
Joseph explained to him that the three

branches were three days. In three days
the Pharaoh would set the cupbearer free,
pardon him and give him back his job.
Joseph asked the man to remember him
when he was freed, tell the Pharaoh
about him and ask for his release.

The chief baker then told Joseph about his dream,
"I was carrying three bread baskets on my head. The top one held pastries for the Pharaoh and the birds were eating them."
Joseph explained that the three baskets were three days. In three days the Pharaoh would release him and hang him from a tree. Birds would peck at him.

Three days later the Pharaoh gave
a banquet. He released the cupbearer and
gave him back his job, but he killed the
baker. It all happened just as Joseph had
said, but the cupbearer forgot about him.

Two years passed. One night, the
Pharaoh had a dream that worried him.
He dreamt that he was standing by the
River Nile. Seven fat cows came out of
the river and began to eat the grass. Then
seven more cows came out, but they were
thin and bony, and they ate up the fat
cows. Later the Pharaoh had another
dream. He saw seven ears of corn, plump
and ripe, growing on one stem, then
seven others, thin and scorched by the
wind. The thin ears swallowed up the
plump ones. In the morning the Pharaoh

sent for all the magicians and wise men in Egypt, and told them his dreams. But no-one could explain them. Then the cupbearer remembered Joseph. He told the Pharaoh about the young Hebrew

in prison who explained his own and
the baker's dreams. He reminded the
Pharaoh how things had turned out just
as Joseph said.

The Pharaoh had Joseph brought to him
from prison. "No-one has been able to
explain my dreams, but I'm told that you
can," he said. Joseph replied, "I can't
explain them, but God can."

Then the Pharaoh told Joseph his dreams, and Joseph said:
"These two dreams carry the same message. God is telling you what will happen. The seven fat cows and the seven plump ears of corn are seven good years. The seven thin cows and the seven dried–up ears of corn are seven years of famine.
There will be seven years of great plenty in Egypt. Then there will be seven years of terrible famine, and the good years will be forgotten. You dreamt it twice, showing God means it to happen soon."

And Joseph added,
"The Pharaoh must now choose a wise
and clever man and put him in charge of
the country. During the good years, he
and his helpers will see to it that in every
town around Egypt food is collected and
stored, and guarded. This food will be
kept for the years of famine."

The Pharaoh and his men thought
Joseph's plan was excellent.
"We'll never find a man as wise as
this, with God's spirit in him," said the
Pharaoh. And he put Joseph in charge of
the country, making him governor over
all Egypt. The Pharaoh took the royal
ring from his hand and put it on Joseph's
finger. He dressed him in fine linen robes
and hung a gold chain around his neck.
He gave Joseph a royal chariot to ride
in, and a wife, Asenath, the daughter of
a well-known priest.

Joseph was thirty years old. He travelled
from one town to another, across Egypt,
organising the food stores. For seven
good years, the land produced plentiful
crops. They were collected and stored in
the cities. There was so much corn that
Joseph couldn't measure it – it was like
the sands of the sea.

In these good years, Joseph and Asenath
had two sons: Manasseh and Ephraim.

But the years of plenty came to an end.
The land produced nothing and animals
wasted away. Joseph opened the grain
stores. There was famine everywhere
else, but in Egypt there was food. People
came from all parts to buy corn.
In Canaan too, Jacob heard of the corn
in Egypt, and he sent all his sons, except
Benjamin, the youngest, to buy some and
bring it home. He kept Benjamin with
him because he feared some misfortune.

When Jacob's sons arrived in Egypt,
they bowed down before Joseph to ask
for their rations. They did not recognise
him, but he knew them. He remembered
the dreams of his childhood that had
made them angry.

"Where have you come from?" Joseph
asked them.
"From Canaan," they said, "to buy corn."
Joseph did not want to let them know
who he was. He wanted to test them.
He said, "I don't believe you, I think
you're spies!"

Jacob's sons answered, "No sir, we're not spies, we're just ten brothers come for food. The youngest stayed with our father, and another brother is dead." But Joseph put them all in prison, and after three days he told them, "Go back to Canaan with your corn and fetch your youngest brother to me. This will prove whether or not you are telling

the truth. Meanwhile, I'll keep one of you prisoner here."

The brothers told one another that they were being punished for what they had done to Joseph all those years ago. Joseph heard them, and he went away on his own and wept. Later he went back to his brothers and chose Simeon to be his prisoner.

Joseph gave orders that his brothers'
packs be filled with corn, and food for
their journey. He had their money put
back in their packs too. The nine brothers
loaded up their donkeys and set off for
Canaan.

They stopped for the night, and one
brother opened his pack and found the
money he thought he had paid for the
corn. They were all frightened and
puzzled. What could this mean?

When they arrived home, they told Jacob

what had happened, and how they must return to Egypt with Benjamin, or Simeon would die.

Jacob was now without two of his sons, so he refused to let them take Benjamin. But the famine in Canaan grew worse and worse. Finally all the supplies of corn were used, and Jacob knew that his sons must go back to Egypt for more. Jacob's sons told him, "The governor of Egypt warned us that we can't ask for more corn unless we take Benjamin." Then Judah told his father, "I'll make sure that Benjamin is safe, and I'll bring him back to you alive. Now, we must leave at once."

So Jacob had to agree to the plan.
He told his sons to take gifts for the
governor of Egypt, the best that Canaan
could produce – balsam, honey, spices,
pistachio nuts and almonds...
The nine brothers set off again for Egypt,
this time with Benjamin.
When Joseph saw that they had brought
Benjamin with them, he ordered a rich
feast to be prepared at his house. Then
he set Simeon free.
Meanwhile, the brothers were dreading
what Joseph might do next.
But he came to them and asked,

"You told me about your old father.
How is he these days? Is he still alive?"
"Our father is alive and well," they
replied, bowing to him.
Joseph turned to Benjamin,
"So this is the youngest brother."
And then he hurried away to his room
and wept – he felt moved to see this
brother he loved so much.
When Joseph had washed his face, he
ordered the feast to be served. Benjamin
was given five times as much as the
other brothers.

After the feast, Joseph told his servant, "Fill my brothers' packs with corn, and put their money in the top of the packs. Place my own precious silver cup inside Benjamin's pack, along with his money." The next morning, the brothers heaved their packs onto their donkeys and began their journey. But hardly had they left the city than Joseph made his chief servant run after them and tell them,

"Why have you repaid good with evil? You have stolen my master's silver cup, the one he uses to foretell the future!"

The brothers swore that they were not thieves, that they knew nothing of the cup. They said, "If one of us is found to have it, he must be killed and the rest of us become slaves here."

Then they put their packs on the ground and let the servant search them.

He looked through all the packs,
starting with that of the eldest brother.
Sure enough, the cup was found in
Benjamin's sack. The brothers tore their
clothes in misery. Then they loaded their
donkeys and returned to the city.
They found Joseph in his house, and
bowed before him. Joseph asked them,

"Why did you do this? You must have known that I'm able to see what people do. The one who had the cup will be my slave. The rest of you may return to your father."

Judah replied,
"Please, sir, let me speak with you.
Our father has already lost one son and
hasn't recovered from it. If we arrive
home without his dear Benjamin, he will
die of sadness. Please, keep me as your
slave instead of Benjamin."

Joseph could no longer hide his feelings.
He told all his servants to leave the room,
and he said to his brothers,
"I am Joseph."
They were stunned, and could not speak.
Joseph said kindly,
"Don't be afraid. I am your brother,
Joseph, whom you sold as a slave into
Egypt. In this way, God sent me ahead
of you to rescue you later. God has made
me governor of this country so that
I may help you in this famine."

"Go quickly! Find my father. Tell him to come and live in Egypt, with his children and grandchildren, his sheep, goats and cattle and all he owns. I'll look after everyone here."

Then Joseph threw his arms around Benjamin and they both wept.

When news reached the Pharaoh, he told Joseph, "Your brothers should return to Canaan. When they come back with Jacob and their families, I'll give them the best land in Egypt."

So the brothers went back to Jacob.
When they told him their story, he
exclaimed, "My son Joseph is alive!
I'll see him before I die!"
Jacob took his family and his friends to
Egypt. They travelled with their animals
and everything they owned, in wagons
sent by the Pharaoh. And so it was that
the Hebrews settled in Egypt. Joseph
looked after them, and lived to the age
of a hundred
and ten.

This collection introduces characters and themes that they will come across in art, music and literature, and in everyday language. People have found spiritual insights in the stories for centuries. Our *Best Bible Stories* are retold close to the original scriptures, after comparing several of the most respected translations, including *The Good News Bible* (1994), *The New English Bible* (1970), *The New Jerusalem Bible* (1990) and *The Revised Standard Version* (1973). The aim of this series is to make the stories more accessible and attractive to children, using clear language without stylistic effects or old-fashioned expressions. Occasionally, and to avoid repetition, narrative has been simplified. Long genealogies have been cut out. The only additions are brief explanations of key ideas – what a prophet is, why sacrifices are significant – and these are built into the text.

Jacqueline Vallon, who devised this series, is editor of religious books for children at Gallimard Jeunesse, in France. She also has experience as a teacher of literature and French, and as a journalist specialising in world religions.

Maurice Pommier used to be a sorter with the French postal service. He taught himself to draw and has always created stories with pictures. But it was only when a friend insisted he show his work to a well-known Paris publisher that he embarked on his second career, as an illustrator creating a wide variety of books for children and adults. He is seen here in a self-portrait with a long, Biblical beard.